INTRODUCTION

WHO THIS
BOOK IS FOR

Accounting for Beginners - Accounting Software supplement is for the self-employed, the business owner, the freelancer, who wants to better run their own business, get insight into the inner workings of their business, do their own accounting for their small business or their self employed gig. It is for the unemployed individual who wants to upgrade their skills, learn vital financial skills, or get a better paying office job or remote job. It is for the virtual assistant who wants to offer more options to their clients. It is for the service worker who wants to progressively and gradually upgrade their skills and secure their future.

You should have already learned the basics of manual accounting taught in my book Accounting for Beginners., which is a prerequisite of learning accounting software.

WHY YOU NEED TO
UPGRADE SKILLS

The employment world has drastically changed and continue to change.

Tech changes constantly make some jobs obsolete. The pandemic disrupted whole industries and ended countless jobs and businesses. Service and low-skilled jobs were some of the most heavily impacted.

As we've seen time and again, those who are ahead of the times, those who are aware of the changes and prepare for them, prosper.

HOW TO STUDY THIS BOOK

Learning to use accounting software is easy when you understand that there are a few types of entries you need to make and most of the entries will be these types.

Accounting entries have to do with the functioning of the business. Basically, you have purchases of supplies, purchases of goods for sale, sales to customers, and expense recording..

At the end of the month or quarter or year, you will generate financial statements.

Accounting software lets you generate the different financial statements with a click of the button. Simply, click on the appropriate menu, choose the required financial report, view and analyze it on screen, and print or email if you like.

ACCOUNTING SOFTWARE

There are many accounting software apps or programs available. Some are for expert or complex accounting use. Others are more suitable for new users and home-based business. Some allow online / cloud usage so you don't need to download the software.

Some popular ones are:

- Sage 50 (Formerly Peachtree)
- QuickBooks
- QuickBooks Online
- FreshBooks
- Zero
- Wave

You can take advantage of one month trial periods to practice your skills.

When using accounting software, you need to learn 3 main things:

1. Recording Revenue using the Sales / Invoice function.
2. Recording Purchases of goods for resale, using the Purchases function.
3. Recording Expenses, using General Journal.

GENERAL JOURNAL ENTRIES

Company startup, asset purchases, and expenses are all General Journal Entries.

Note: purchasing assets and office supplies are recorded differently from purchases of goods for resale (discussed later).

On January 1, Aleena started a company with $40,000 investment that she deposited into the company bank account. She rented an office, paying $4,000 rent for three months. In addition, office supplies cost $400 and equipment cost $8,000; and the company website cost $2,500 to make. Advertising expenses were $500. How do you record the transactions in accounting software?

To record the transactions, open the General Journal function from the menu bar.

In the Account field, enter the account number or search for the Cash account and select it.

If the Cash account hasn't been set up, click New to set up the account. You can also create accounts in the Chart of Accounts function. Since cash is an asset account, as with all asset accounts, choose Asset and Permanent (or Account doesn't close) classifications.

Give the account an account number, and save.

Account numbers and chart of accounts are discussed in my book Accounting for Beginners.

To recall: Assets are given account numbers starting with 1, Liabilities, 2, Capital Accounts 3, Revenue 4, and Expenses 5.

General Journal Entries Continued

Once the account is set up and saved, ensure that the cash account number is in the account number field in the General Journal. Then add the date of the transaction, a description in the description field, and the amount $40,000 in the debit column. In the next line, do the same for the Capital (or Equity) account. Set up the account, enter the account number in the account number field. and enter $40,000 in the credit column. This records the first transaction. Click Save to save the transaction.

Note: The Cash Account shows the total cash balance, including the the cash on hand and the bank account balances.

Repeat the same method for the remaining transactions, creating accounts as needed.

Debit Prepaid Rent (an asset account) for $4000 and credit Cash for $4000

Debit Office Supplies for $400 / Credit Cash $400.

Debit Office Equipment (an asset account) for $8000 and credit Cash for $8000 .

Branding Costs - Debit Company Website (an asset account)$2500 / credit Cash $2500 .

Debit Advertising expenses $500 and credit Cash $500

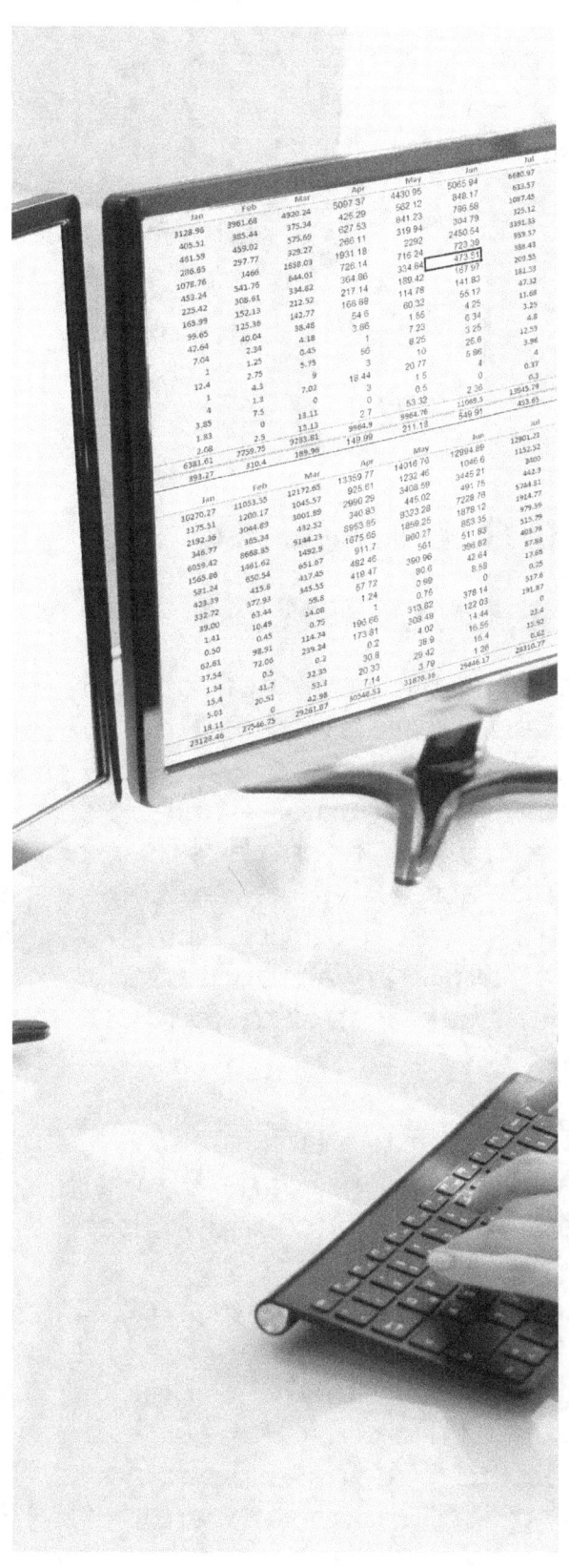

Classification of Accounts:

There are several classification of accounts in the double entry accounting system.
There are nominal accounts and permanent accounts.

Nominal accounts close at the end of each accounting fiscal period. An example is the revenue account and expense accounts.

Permanent accounts don't close but remain open throughout the life of the business. Assets, liabilities, and Capital are permanent accounts.

In accounting software, when adding capital accounts, it's necessary to set them as equity that closes (Dividends Account) or equity that doesn't close. When the software closes the books, accounts that need to be closed will close automatically.

Another classification is the category an account belongs to, such as Assets, Expenses, Revenue, Capital, of Liabilities.

What are nominal and permanent accounts?

Some accounts are closed at the end of each fiscal year, with the balance being transferred to other (permanent) accounts. These include revenue, expense, and owner drawing accounts. Other accounts remain open for as long as the business is in existence. These include assets, liability, and capital. The income summary account (used in manual accounting) is a temporary account used to close and transfer account balances at the end of the accounting cycle.

Nominal accounts are closed at the end of each accounting year so that the accounts can start with a zero balance at the start of each accounting fiscal period (and show only the balances for that particular year). This aids in business analysis and decision making.

Accounting software does the closing functions automatically when it closes the books for a particular accounting period. This makes keeping accounting records using accounting software easier.

RECORDING INVENTORY PURCHASES FOR RESALE

Inventory purchased for resale and other asset purchases are recorded differently.

Purchases of inventory for resale is recorded using the Purchases function. The Purchases and supplier functions are used for recording items related to resale only (and not to record office supplies, which is recorded through the general journal function.)
Note: these are called Purchases.

To record the purchases, click on "Purchases" on the menu bar and choose the supplier / vendor account to which you want to add the entry. If there is no supplier account, create a New Supplier using the New function on the purchase invoice or choose Supplier from the menu bar.

RECORDING INVENTORY PURCHASES FOR RESALE

Example: The company bought $20,000 worth of goods from ABC Suppliers (a long term supplier), paying 50% in advance and 50% due in 30 days. The company also bought $5000 worth of goods from FirstCo, a new supplier, paying cash.

Record the entries using accounting software.

To record the purchase from ABC Suppliers, open Purchase Orders and choose ABC Suppliers from the supplier / vendor list. Then record the purchase, entering the details of the purchase, quantity, and total amount due.

If there is a space for advance payment, enter the amount paid here. If not, then save the transaction. Then open Payments from the menu bar, select ABC Suppliers in Vendors ID, choose the purchase invoice, and enter the advance payment amount.

To record the purchase from FirstCo, click on Suppliers/Vendors in the Maintain menu bar, click Add New, and enter the supplier details. Then go to Purchases, and record the purchase transaction.

If there is no cash payment option, save the purchase invoice Then click on Payments menu to record the advance payment..

RECORDING SALES

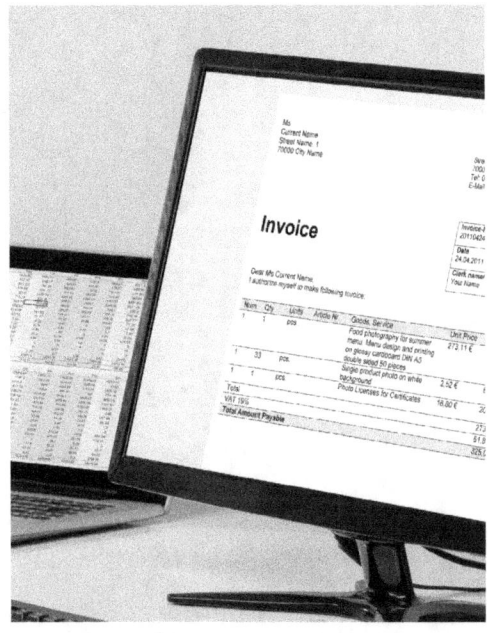

IT ALL STARTS WITH THE CUSTOMER

Recording sales using accounting software:

The company had sales of $4000, cash receipts of $2000, and sales returns of $1000. How do you record the transactions? Assume all sales are made on account.

In accounting software, you don't need to go through the general journal when recording these transactions. Sales are recorded using the sales and invoicing function.

To record this type of transaction in accounting software, you will first create the customer account, from the Customer option on the Maintain menu bar.

Then click on Sales/Invoices to record the sale.

Alternately, you can also click on Sales/Invoice function, choose the Customer name from the list and complete the entry.

If the customer account isn't there, click "New" and create the customer account from the Sales/Invoice page.

All sales entries are "on account" by default. If your accounting software allows you enter the cash payment amount on the invoice page, click "Amount paid at sale" and enter it.

If not, or you need to record payment from customer at a later date, click on the "Receipts" function in the Task menu , choose the receipt number / customer name from the list, and record the transaction.

Note: Receipts are payments from customers and "Payments" are payments to suppliers.

169,02
95,25
24,78
67,41
69,68
72,82
220,91
69,60

56,19
58,73
178,15
56,13

0,00

RECORDING SALES RETURNS

In accounting software, a sales returns transaction is recorded using the Credit Memo Function.

Sales Returns are recorded using a separate account because it helps management make important decisions regarding the business. For example, if management sees the sales returns are too high, management can look into the reasons for this high returns rate and make changes. At the time of the sales returns, click on Credit Memo function from the Tasks bar, choose the customer name from the list, select the invoice number, and enter details of the sales return or refund.

RECORDING EXPENSE PAYMENTS

TAKE CARE OF YOUR PEOPLE AND THEY WILL TAKE CARE OF YOUR CUSTOMERS

Payments for expenses need to be done on time and without delay or reminders from the creditor.

Expense payments include:
- Salaries & Wages Expense
- Utilities Expenses
- Rent Expense
- Advertising Expense
- Commission Expense
- Tax Expense

To record these, on the accounting software, you will use the general journal function.

You will first create separate accounts for each expense item. Then when the expense is incurred, open General Journal. In Account Number, click the dropdown menu to open the list and choose the appropriate expense account (or enter the account number if you know it). Enter the date of the transaction, enter the description, and enter the amount to be debited. (Note: expense is a debit balance).

Then on the next line, choose the account(s) to be credited from the list. This may be the cash account (if paying in cash) or the payable account (if the payment will be done at a later date, such as salaries payable, tax payable, etc.) In the case of rent, it may be the prepaid rent account.

Enter the details to complete the transaction.

When should expenses and revenue be recorded?

Expenses and revenue should be recorded when incurred, not necessarily when cash is exchanged. This is important for associating the expenses and revenue to the period they were incurred. This is why there are accounts such as Prepaid Expense (an asset account showing payment for an expense not yet incurred) and Deferred Revenue (income received but not yet earned).

Prepaid Expenses are asset accounts and Deferred Revenue are liability accounts.

An Example of prepaid expense is Prepaid Rent paid for 3 months, 6 months, or a year in advance. The accounting entry for prepaid rent is : debit prepaid rent, credit cash. The adjusting entry for recording rent expense is: debit rent expense and credit prepaid rent. In accounting software, use the general journal function to record transactions related to rent expense, including adjusting entries.

RECORDING ADJUSTING ENTRIES

ADJUSTING ENTRIES BRING THE ACCOUNT BALANCES UP TO DATE.

Examples of accounts that you would use adjusting entries with are:

- The supplies Account
- Prepaid Rent / Rent Expense Accounts
- Salaries Payable Account

Example:
Beginning supplies account balance: $50
Supplies purchased on December 2: $150
Ending Supplies Account balance: $65

In this case, we need to know the amount of supplies expense. We calculate as follows: Beginning balance $50 + purchases $150 - ending balance $65 = supplies used (supplies expense) $135. To record the adjusting entry: Debit Supplies Expense for $135 Credit Supplies for $135

In accounting software, use the General Journal function to make the entries to the supplies account.

The reason for using the General Journal and not the Purchases function is that we are working with the Office Supplies account

(operational expense) and not the Inventory account.

Note: .Supplies is an Asset account. When office supplies are purchased, the supplies account is debited. At the end of the month, supplies on hand are calculated and the necessary adjusting entry is made to record supplies expense.

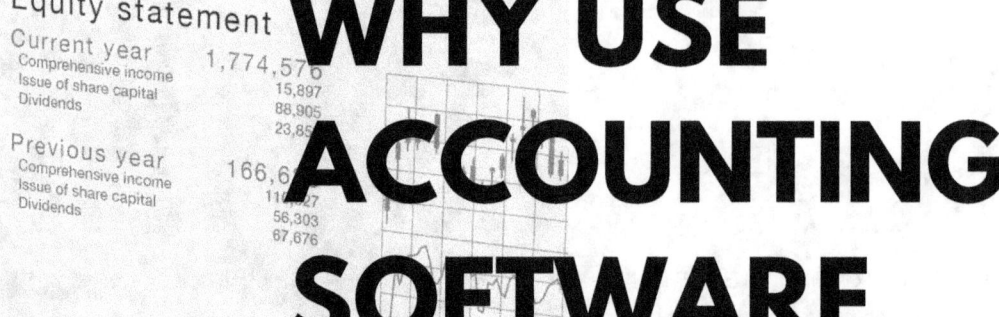

WHY USE ACCOUNTING SOFTWARE

Equity statement
Current year 1,774,576
Comprehensive income
Issue of share capital 15,897
Dividends 88,905
23,85

Previous year 166,6
Comprehensive income
Issue of share capital 11 27
Dividends 56,303
67,676

Cash flow statement
Operations
Net earnings 12,978,516
Depreciation 12,873,892
104,624

Investing
Real estate 6,372,535
Equipment 1,385,395
4,439,118

Financing
Notes payable 6,505,981
6,505,981

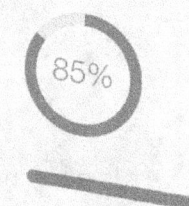

85%

Accounting software makes the accounting process a piece of cake. With accounting software, you only need to record the transactions. The posting to ledgers, closing, and financial statement preparation are done automatically or with the click of a button.

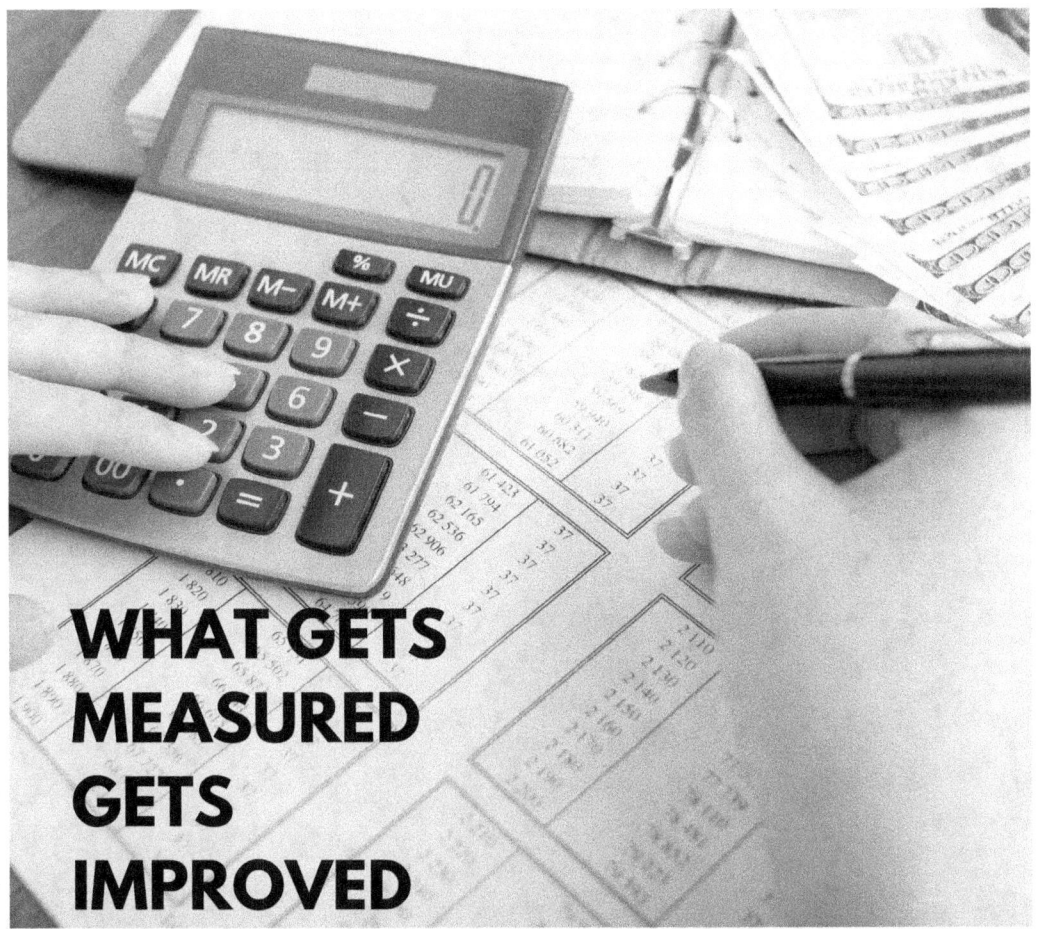

WHAT GETS MEASURED GETS IMPROVED

IMPORTANT FINANCIAL REPORTS

After you have completed recording transactions or at the end of the financial period, you will generate financial reports.

The Trial Balance

The Trial Balance is prepared to check the accuracy of the financial records. The trial balance checks that total debits equal total credits. If this isn't the case, it means there is an error in the records which needs to be found and fixed before continuing. To create the Trial Balance, click on Reports & Forms, General Ledger, and choose General Ledger Trial Balance.

INCOME STATEMENT

REVENUES
Gross Revenues

EXPENSES
Materials
Subcontractors
Utilities
Advertising
Entertainment

889,1

223,200
264,000
4,473
18,900
16,65
7,5

The other financial reports you will make are:

- The Balance Shoot
- The Income Statement
- Stockholders / Owners Equity Statement
- The Statement of Cash Flows

These financial statements are made monthly, quarterly, biannually, or at least once annually.

To create the financial reports in accounting software, click Reports and Forms (or similar menu item). Click "Financial Statements," choose the type of financial statement you want to make, and double-click it. if there is an option for time period or date range, enter it (such as current period or other date range.
Click ok to complete. You may now view, save, print, and email the report.

Note: menu item names may differ in different accounting programs.

ACCOUNTING FOR BEGINNERS

ACCOUNTING SOFTWARE SUPPLEMENT

AUTHOR'S NOTE

I hope you benefited a great deal.

Dear reader, It was a pleasure writing this book. I hope I was able to convey the content in clear terms. If there is something you didn't understand, want to be elaborated on, or added, feel free to email me at kokab@radeya.biz When the book is updated, you will get an updated e-book copy for free. I would appreciate if you leave a review to help others with their buying decisions. Finally, be sure to checkout my other books from Amazon.

~Kokab Rahman

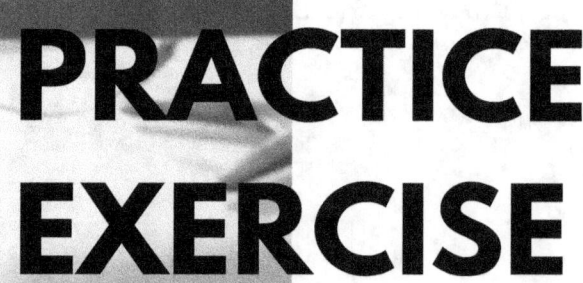

PRACTICE EXERCISE

Education is the passport to the future, for tomorrow belongs to those who prepare for it today.
~ Malcolm X

On March 1, the business owners started the company, Empire Construction, depositing $150,000 in the company bank account. Record the transaction.

Create the necessary accounts, using Chart of Accounts Function in the accounting software:

Assets
Cash 1100
Accounts Receivable 1200
Office Supplies 1300
Prepaid Rent 1400
Equipment 1800

Liabilities
Accounts Payable 2100
Salaries Payable 2200
Debt Payable 2300
Tax Payable 2900

Capital
Owner's Equity 3100
Retained Earnings 3200

Revenue
Construction Services 4100
Product Sales 4200

Expenses
Rent Expense 5100
Salaries Expense 5200
Utilities Expense 5300
Office Supplies Exp 5400
Misc. Expense 5800
Tax Expense 5900

When creating new accounts, make sure to use the correct classification (assets, capital, etc. and permanent or temporary).

To record the transaction in General Journal:

Open General Journal.
Click the search icon in the Account number field and select the Cash account.
Press enter to enter the account number in the General Journal entry.
Complete the debit entry entering, date, description, and debit amount of $150,000.

On the next line, in the account number field, click the search icon and select the Owner's Equity account. Press enter to enter the account number in the General Journal. Complete the credit entry fields.

Click save to save the transaction.

Note: the date to enter in the entry is the date of the transaction, as evidenced by the invoice or receipt.

On March 1, paid rent for 1 month, $10,000.

Open General Journal.
Complete the line for the debit entry, debiting the Rent Expense account $10,000.

Then complete the line for the credit entry, crediting the Cash account for $10,000.

When all fields are filled in, click save.

*Note: Because the rent paid is for one month only, we debited Rent Expense directly instead of using the Prepaid Rent account.

On March 2, bought office equipment on account for $5000. from JP Associates. Payment due in 90 days.

For this transaction, we use the General Journal instead of the Purchases Function because the purchase is not for inventory for resale.

To record the transaction, open General Journal.

In the first line, enter the debit entry information, debiting the Office Equipment account for $5000.

In the second line, enter the credit entry information, crediting the Accounts Payable account for $5000.

Hint: the best way to do these exercise questions is to attempt them yourself using an accounting program, then check with the answers to check your answer.

On March 5, paid 3 months Advertising & Marketing Expense, $18,000.

Solution: Because we don't have the required accounts for this transaction, we will create the Prepaid Advertising account, an asset account, and the Advertising Expense account from the Chart of Accounts and give them appropriate account numbers in line with our list of previously made accounts.

Then, in the General Journal function, complete the debit entry, debiting Prepaid Advertising, and the credit entry, crediting the Cash account, for the $18000.
Enter all the details (Account numbers, date, description, and debit and credit amounts),. Then click save.

Open the Customers Function and create a Customer Account for Paulo Properties.

On March 15, received a contract for construction services from Paulo Properties for $40,000. Paulo Properties paid 50% in advance and the balance to be paid after 30 days.

Enter the Customer Account number, company name, and other details, and click save.

Then open the Sales / Invoice function and create the invoice to record the transaction.

Enter Customer ID / Account number (or click the search icon and choose the appropriate customer account from the list of customers.

Enter the date of the transaction, invoice number, and other details related to payment requirements.

Enter total revenue amount $40,000., and amount paid at the time of sale, $20,000.

In payment terms, enter "Due in 30 days."

Check to see the information is correct, then click Save.

March 31, adjusting entry for prepaid advertising expense.

Prepaid advertising equaled $18,000 for 3 months.

At the end of March, one month of advertising expense was used. This equals $6000.
Calculations: $18,000 / 3 months = $6000 per month.

To record the adjusting entry, open the General Journal.
Debit Advertising Expense for $6000.
Credit Prepaid Advertising for $6000.

Ensure all the debit and credit accounts information, date, and amounts are entered and accurate. Then click Save.

On March 31, Paulo Properties paid the remaining amount due after all services were provided to the customer.

To record the transaction, open Receipts and choose the Customer ID. From the list, choose the appropriate customer Invoice number.

Record the payment details.

Note: When using the Sales Invoice/Receipts and Purchases/Payments functions, the accounting software does the other half of the accounting entry on the back end, crediting or debiting the cash account as required by the transaction.

March 31, paid salaries to Joe ($7000), Martin ($4000), and Sam ($8000).

To record the salaries payment / payroll transaction, open General Journal and enter the transaction details, debiting each worker's Salaries Expense account for the given amount and crediting Cash for the total.

Since we don't have the individual worker's salary account, we will create them now.

Click the search icon in the account number field.

Create new accounts with the worker's names and the account numbers 5201, 5202, and 5203. Select the Expense classification for each account.

Once each account is created and saved, on the General Journal, in the first 3 lines, enter each account information and debit amount. In the 4th line, enter the Cash account's information and credit amount for the total salaries expense.

In accounting software, you can also use the Payroll Function to handle salaries. However, we will not cover such advanced topics in this book.

On April 1, paid rent for 1 month, $10,000.

Use the General Journal to record Rent Expense transaction, debiting Rent Expense and crediting the Cash account.

You may have to record payroll taxes, income tax, sales tax, and VAT tax in your accounting / bookkeeping work, depending on your state / country laws. Taxes are recorded as a debit to tax expense and credit to cash or taxes payable.

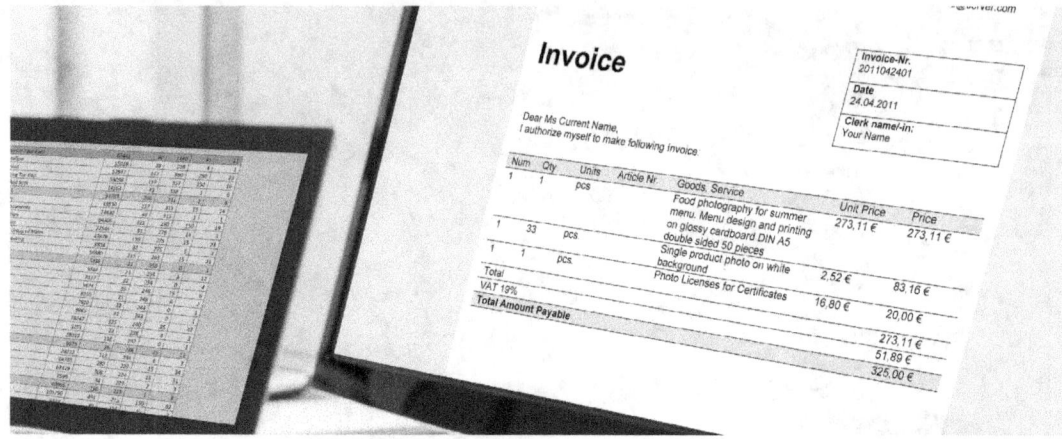

On April 3, purchased Italian marble blocks from KingsView Marbles for $55,000 to be sold to customers. Paid in cash. Profit Margin on these is 50%.

Since we are purchasing inventory for resale, we will use the Purchases Function to record the transaction.

First, create the Supplier Account in the Supplier/Vendor function. Enter the account number, account name, and other details. Then click save.

Create the purchase invoice using the Purchases function.

On the purchase invoice, in Account ID, use the search icon to find the supplier account. Press enter to enter the account information in the invoice.

Enter the purchase details, description, quantity, and cost.

Enter amount paid in cash. ($55,000) If there is no such option, save the invoice.

Go to the Payments Function, open the invoice you want to pay. Enter the payment amount and click save.

On April 10, sold half the marble to Alpha Homes at 2X the purchase price. Payment due in 1 week.

Create the customer account using the Customer function. Enter customer account number, company name, and other details.

Record the sale on account using the sales/invoice function.

Open Sales/Invoice. Enter the customer ID or choose from the list using the search icon.

Enter the sales details, amount and payment terms (Due in 1 Week).

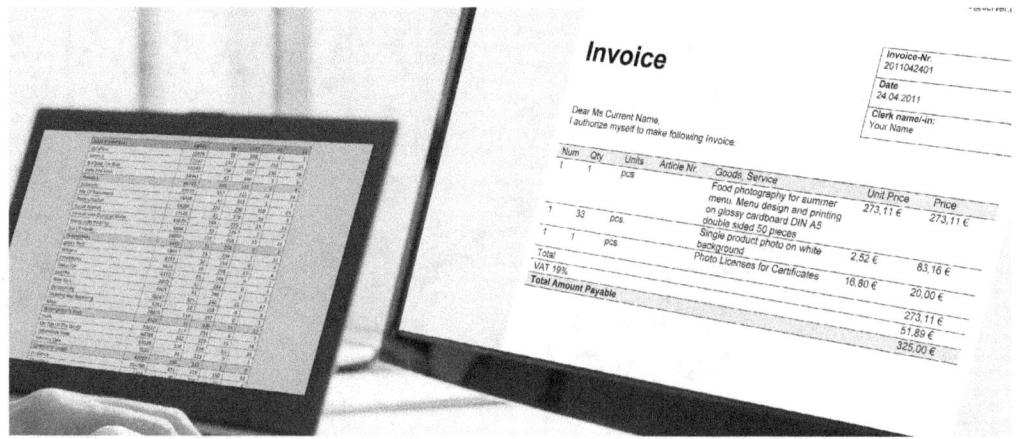

Hint: Amount owed is $55,000.
Calculations: the full load of marble wholesale cost was $55,000. The company sold half of it, with a wholesale price of $27,500.
Since the company has a 50% profit margin rule, it means the company sold the marble at 2X the price = $55,000 retail price.

On April 17, Alpha Homes paid the amount owed in full. Create the payment receipt transaction.

Go to the Receipts function. Open the relevant invoice using customer ID / Invoice number .

Hint: use the search icon in invoice ID to find the customer account and invoice.

Enter the payment details, $55,000 cash payment.

Click save.

On April 20, Alpha Homes returned 10% of the marble. Create the Credit Memo for $5,500 recording the return.

In the accounting software, open the Credit Memo function.

Find the affected customer account and open the relevant invoice.

Enter the date and other details of the sales return or refund.

You can use online profit margin calculators to find out the retail price, wholesale price, profit margin, etc. of a product.

On April 24, sold the remaining marble in inventory to BZ Homes. Received payment in cash ($60,500). Note: this includes the marble returned by Alpha Homes.

Create the new customer account using the Customer function.

Record the sales transaction using the sales/invoicing function..

Enter the cash receipt information, amount paid at time of sale = $60,500.

On April 25, paid commission expense of $6500

Record the transaction using the General Journal.

Create the Commission Expense account.

Then complete the General Journal entry, debiting Commissions Expense for $6500 and crediting cash for $6500.

Save the transaction.

On April 25, paid commission expense of $6500

Record the transaction using the General Journal.

Create the Commission Expense account.
Then complete the General Journal entry, debiting Commissions Expense for $6500 and crediting cash for $6500.
Save the transaction.

There is no payroll tax paid on commission expense or payments to independent contractors for services provided.

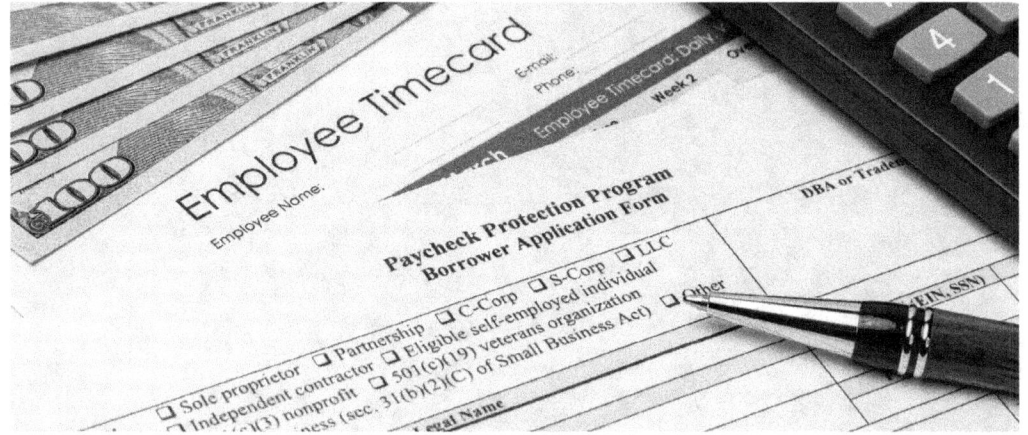

On April 30, paid salaries to employees Joe ($7500), Martin ($8000), Sam ($8500), and Jane ($6000). Also paid cleaning service fees, $2000.
Hint: Record all using the General Journal.

Open General Journal.

As before, in one journal entry, record the salaries expense transactions, debiting individual worker salary expense accounts and crediting the Cash account.

Create new accounts where needed.

Check that all the information is included and accurate. Then save the General Journal Entry.

To record the cleaning services fees, click New General Journal entry.

Create the Cleaning Expense account.

Complete the General Journal entry, debiting Cleaning Expense and crediting Cash.

On April 30, create the adjusting entry for advertising expense.

In General Journal, debit Advertising Expense and credit Prepaid Advertising for $6,000.

Schooling doesn't ensure employment but skill does.

~Amit Kalantri, Wealth of Words

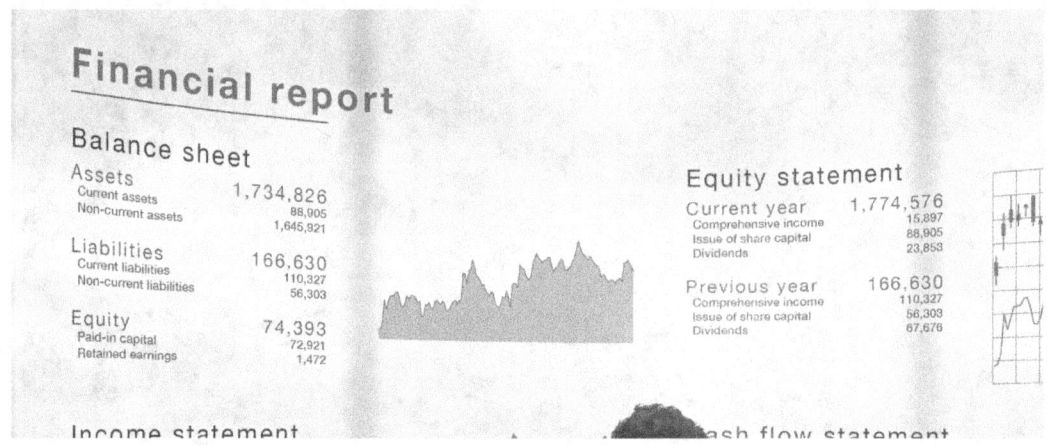

Create the Balance Sheet for March 1

Accounting software makes generating financial reports and financial statements easy. To create a financial statement such as the balance sheet, go to Forms & Reports.

Click on Financial Statements.
Choose Balance Sheet from the list and double click it.
Enter the date, period, or date range. Then click ok.
You can now view, save, print and email your financial report.

Empire Construction
Balance Sheet
March 1, 20XX

Assets	**Liabilities & Owners Equity**
Cash $150,000	Liabilities: $0
	Owner's Equity: $150,000
Total Assets:. $150,000	Total Liabilities & Owner's Equity: $150,000

Note: the balance sheet shows the financial position of a company on a given date. For this reason, it's header states the date and doesn't state "for the period ended...."

Create the Income Statement for March 31

To create the income statement, using accounting software, go to Forms & Reports. Click on Financial Statements.

Choose Income Statement from the list and double click it.

Enter the date, period, or date range. Then click ok.

You can now view, save, print and email your financial report.

Empire Construction

Income Statement

For the Month Ended March 31, 20XX

Revenue:

Construction Services Revenue::		$40,000
Construction Premium Product Sales:		$0
Net: Revenue:		$40,000

Expenses:

Rent Expense	$10,000	
Salaries Expense:	19,000	
Advertising Expense:	6,000	
Total Expenses		($35,000)
Net Income		$5000

Note: the income statement shows the revenue and expenses of a business for a specific period of time.

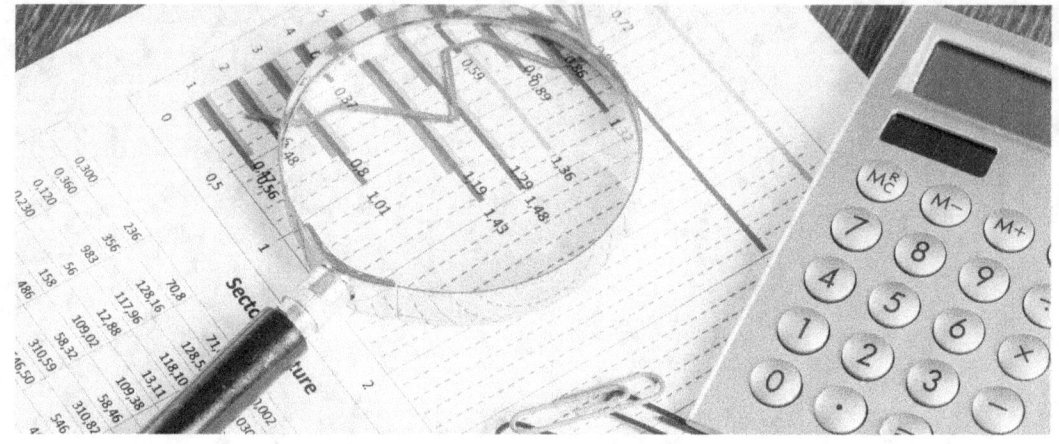

Create the Balance Sheet for April 30

Empire Construction
Balance Sheet
March 1, 20XX

Assets

Cash $149,500

Office Equipment $5000

Prepaid Advertising: $6000

Accounts Receivable: $0

Liabilities & Owners Equity

Liabilities:

Accounts Payable: $5000

Owner's Equity:

Capital: $150,000

Retained Earnings: $5500

Total Assets:. $160,500

Total Liabilities & Owner's Equity: $160,500

Create the Income Statement for April 30

Empire Construction
Income Statement
For the Period Ended April 30, 20XX

Revenue:

Construction Services Revenue::	$40,000	
Construction Premium Product Sales:	$110,000	
Net: Revenue:		$150,000
Cost of Goods Sold:	($55,000)	
Gross Profit:		$95,000

Expenses:

Rent Expense	$20,000	
Salaries Expense:	49,000	
Advertising Expense:	12,000	
Commission Expense:	6500	
Cleaning Expense:	2000	
Total Expenses		($144,500)
Net Income		$5500

Note: numbers in parentheses mean minus or negative.

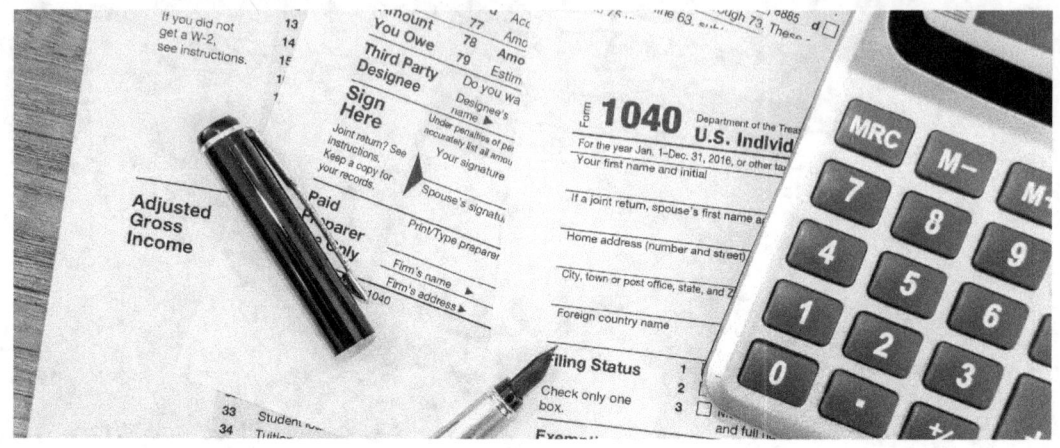

On Tax Expense

There are many types of taxes that will affect a business's accounting records. Different countries and areas have different types of taxes and tax rates. These include:: income tax, payroll tax, sales tax, VAT tax, tax on capital gains, corporate tax, personal income tax, medicare tax, social security tax, and so on.

There are also tax deductions and tax benefits that may benefit you and reduce the amount of tax you pay.

Payroll Tax / Employee Tax

Payroll Taxes are called tax withholdings, which is the percentage of an employee's salary paid in tax. Although the employer pays this tax, it is withheld from the employee's salary. In some places, the employer needs to match the employee tax amount, such as social security tax.

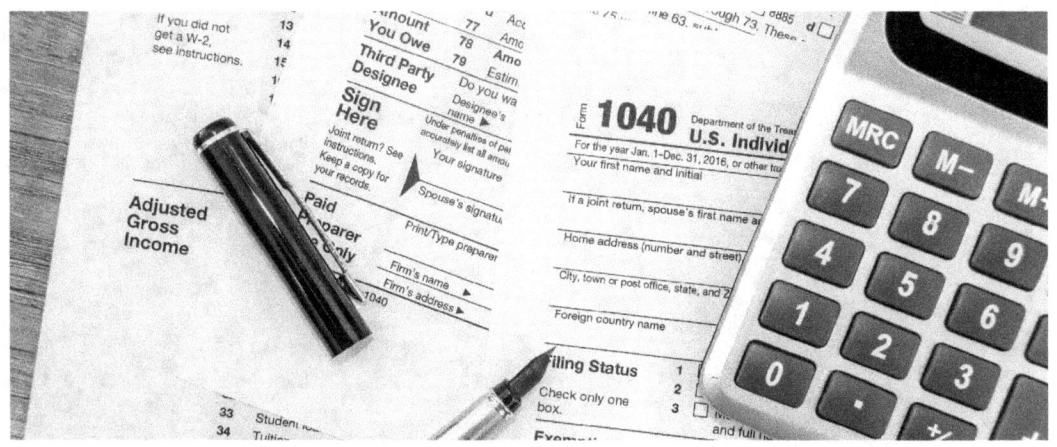

Income Tax

Income tax is paid on the business's profits. Different types of businesses are taxed differently. Taxes need to be paid on time, otherwise the business / individual may incur large penalties.

It is important to know the tax laws of your country / state and ensure proper and timely accounting and payment to avoid penalty.

A company can have a net loss as well. Net Loss means the company's expenses were greater than its revenue. Net Loss is denoted with parentheses on the income statement, meaning it is a negative number. One year's net loss may reduce the following year's tax obligation. Speak to a tax advisor to know more.

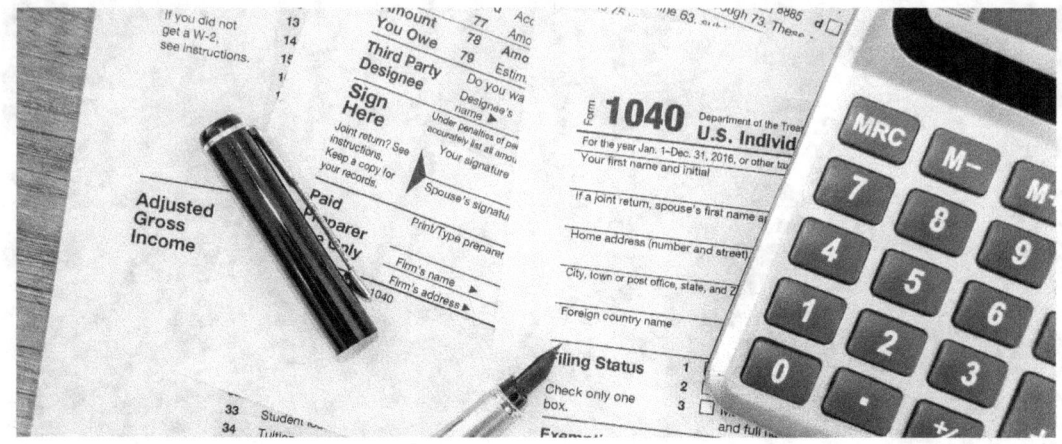

The following year, the business showed a profit of $145,000. Tax rate is 20%. Calculate and record the tax expense, assuming it will be paid end of May.

Income tax expense is calculated and paid annually.

Calculate tax expense: $145,000 X 20% = $29,000

Create the Income Tax Expense and Income Tax Payable accounts.

Record the transaction in the General Journal, debiting Income Tax expense for $29,000, and crediting Income Tax Payable for $29,000.

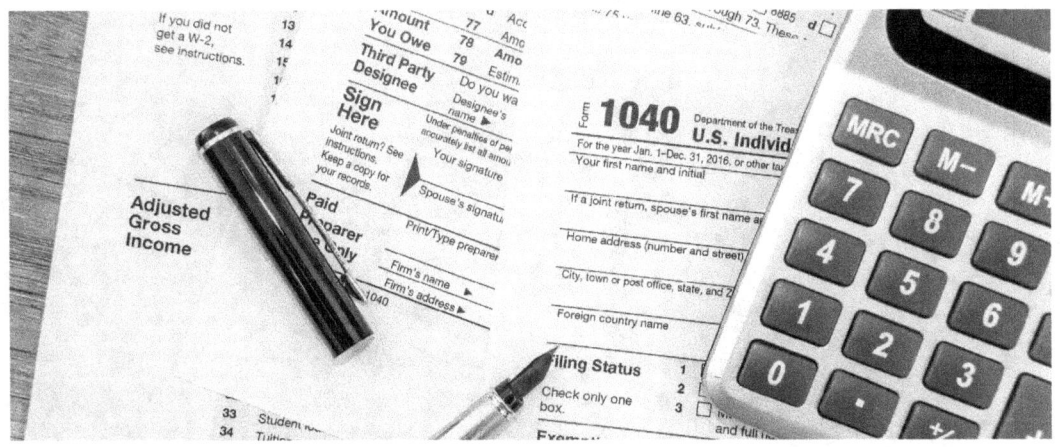

Create the income statement after recording income tax expense.

Simplified income statement:

Empire Construction

Income Statement

For the Year Ended Feb 28, 20XX

Net Revenue:	**$XXXXXXX**
Operational Expenses:	(<u>$XXXXXX)</u>
Income before taxes:	<u>$145,000</u>
Tax expense (20%)	<u>($29,000)</u>
Net Income	<u>$116,000</u>

Note: When you record tax expense in accounting software, the financial reports are automatically affected.

On Depreciation Expense

No asset (other than land) lasts forever. Eventually, assets lose their functionality and value and become worthless.

The way to convert the assets on a business's books to expense is through the gradual recording of depreciation expense.

Accounting standards and tax laws provide the guidelines on the number of years a particular asset class is useful. An asset may be functional longer than that. However, for tax and accounting reporting purposes, the asset is depreciated in that many years.

To calculate the depreciation expense, it's total purchase price is divided on the number of useful years. This gives you the annual depreciation expense.

(Purchase price includes the total amount paid to buy, receive, and install the asset, including amount paid for delivery.

Every year a percentage is used to determine the depreciation expense amount to record.

Depreciation expense reduces the net income of a company and also reduces the amount of tax the company pays.

Important Terms:
Useful Life of an asset: the number of years an asset is expected to be functional.

Residual Value: the amount an asset is expected to sell for after its useful life ends.

In December, the company determined that the equipment bought in March would have a useful life of 5 years and residual value of 0. Calculate and record the depreciation expense for 1 year.

Equipment Price: $5000

Useful life: 5 years

Residual value: 0

Annual depreciation expense: $1000

Calculation: $5000 / 5 years = $1000 depreciation expense per year.

To record depreciation expense, first create Depreciation Expense account from the Chart of Accounts.
Then in the General Journal, enter the transaction entry, debiting Depreciation Expense for $1000, and crediting the Equipment Account for $1000.

Note: Depreciation expense reduces the asset account but doesn't result in a cash outflow.

*Those who take action
see change.*
~ Kokab Rahman

END NOTE

From the author

I want to thank you for taking the initiative to pick up this book and to have the resolve to reach the end. Most people are good at starting things but not at finishing them. You've shown that you're different. That you want to make a difference in your own life and in the lives of your loved ones. I believe in you, that as you continue your journey, you will see progress, by God's Grace.

Finally, I want to add that the names of people, transactions, and businesses used in this book are entirely fictional. and made up Any similarity with actual people, entities, or events are purely coincidental.. The content presented is for education purpose only. Always check your local accounting regulations and tax principles that affects your accounting records. Speak to a tax advisor / financial advisor if unsure.

ACCOUNTING SOFTWARE SUPPLEMENT

ACCOUNTING SOFTWARE SUPPLEMENT

ACCOUNTING SOFTWARE
SUPPLEMENT

www.ingramcontent.com/pod-product-compliance
Lightning Source LLC
Chambersburg PA
CBHW081419220526
45467CB00009B/2738